PRAISE FOR

ABCs

★★★ OF THE ★★★

AIR FORCE

"This *ABCs of the Air Force* will help my grandchildren know what I'm talking about when I say 'the Air Force.' What a great tribute to the 70th anniversary!"

- **Mark D. Stillwagon,** *Brigadier General, USAF-Retired (former Assistant Director of Intelligence, Headquarters U.S. European Command)*

"Every parent will enjoy sharing the *ABCs of the Air Force* with their kids."

- **Jack C. Schofield,** *Colonel, USAF - Retired (former F-16 pilot)*

"The *ABCs of the Air Force* depicts some of our vital missions from a kid's perspective. It should be on every American's coffee table!"

- **James K. Brydon,** *Lieutenant Colonel, USAF- Retired (former Air Force Two Navigator)*

Dedication

To all the Airmen past, present, and future who have performed "eyes right," adjusted their gig line, and eaten in an Open Mess, this book is for you to read to your children and grandchildren. AIM HIGH!

www.mascotbooks.com

ABCs of the Air Force

For more information, please contact:
Mascot Books
620 Herndon Parkway #320
Herndon, VA 20170
info@mascotbooks.com

Library of Congress Control Number: 2017913674

CPSIA Code: PRT1017A
ISBN-13: 978-1-68401-332-6
Printed in the United States

ABCs

✭✭✭ OF THE ✭✭✭

AIR FORCE

Richard Lee Marsh   Illustrations by Jason Bach

A

is for AIRMEN

Twenty-four hours a day and seven days a week, Airmen stand alert, ready to support and defend the United States of America.

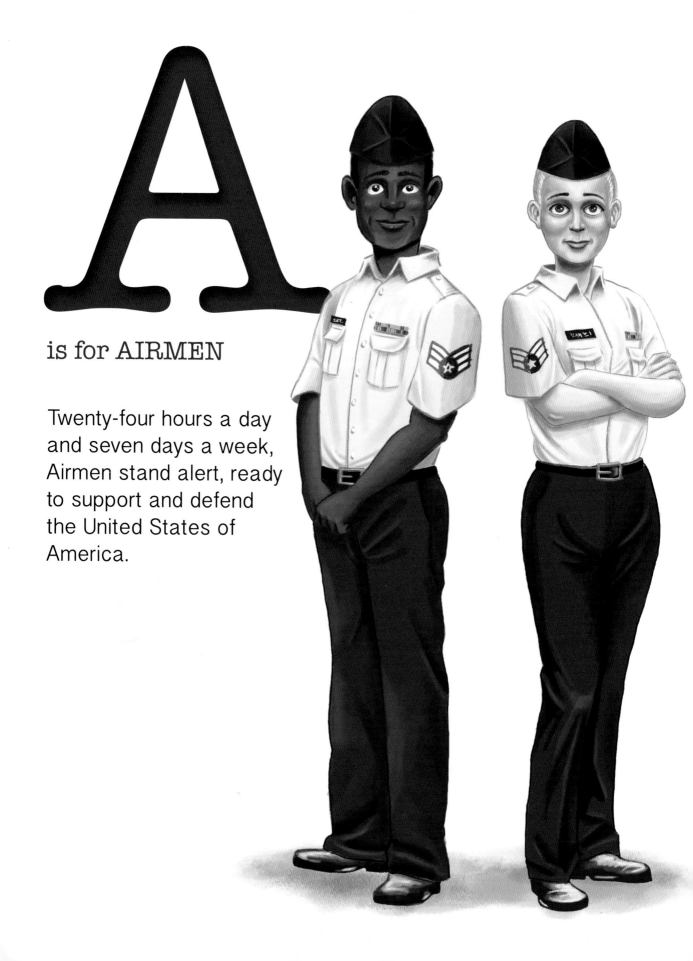

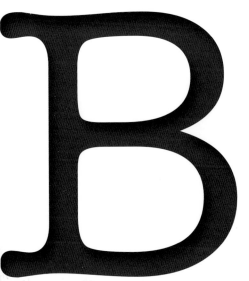

is for BMTS (Basic Military Training School)

BMTS is where new members of the Air Force go to train and learn. For 60 days, they practice marching, saluting, and working together as a Flight of Airmen.

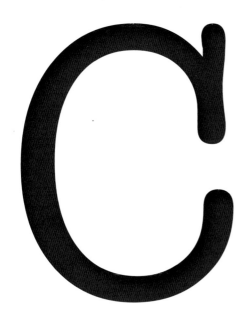

C

is for AIRMAN'S CREED

"I am an American Airman.
I am a Warrior.
I have answered my Nation's call.
I am an American Airman.
My mission is to Fly, Fight, and Win.
I am faithful to a Proud Heritage,
A Tradition of Honor,
And a Legacy of Valor.
I am an American Airman.
Guardian of Freedom and Justice,
My Nation's Sword and Shield,
Its Sentry and Avenger.
I defend my Country with my Life.
I am an American Airman.
Wingman, Leader, Warrior.
I will never leave an Airman behind,
I will never falter,
And I will not fail."

D

is for DEPENDENT

A dependent is a member of the Airman's family who is not in the military, but depends on their Airman. This could be a husband, wife, or even a kid!

E is for E-4

When the president, vice president, or the secretary of defense needs an emergency flying office, the Air Force provides an E-4 plane for them. But the E-4 only has a special name when the president is on board: "Air Force One."

F

is for FIRE

When local fire fighters need help with wildfires, they call the Air Force. The Airmen use special planes with special equipment to put out the fire. These planes can drop 3,000 gallons of water on a wildfire!

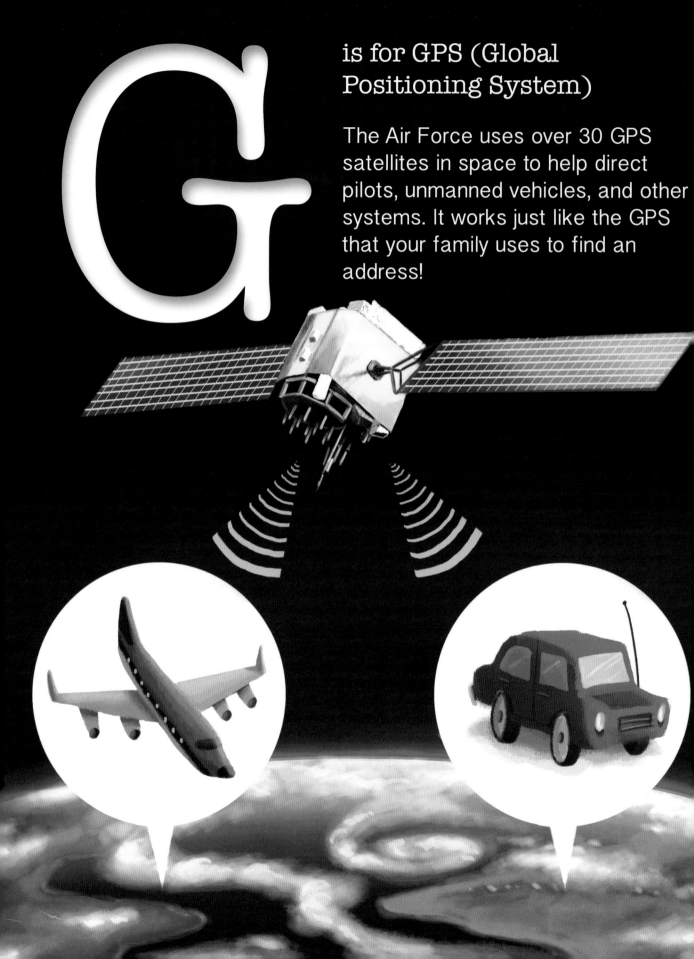

G

is for GPS (Global Positioning System)

The Air Force uses over 30 GPS satellites in space to help direct pilots, unmanned vehicles, and other systems. It works just like the GPS that your family uses to find an address!

H

s for HUMANITARIAN

The Air Force operates the world's largest, fastest, and most advanced fleet of humanitarian aircraft used to deliver life-saving supplies. They airdrop food, water, and medical supplies from 30,000 feet to those in need!

I is for IN-FLIGHT REFUELING

When Air Force aircraft need extra fuel for long flights, flying tankers provide in-flight refueling. That way, aircraft can fly farther without landing.

J

is for JOINT OPERATION

A joint operation is one in which members of more than one Service work together. The Air Force performs joint missions with the Army, Navy, and the Marines. The Joint Chiefs of Staff are the top leaders of the four Services.

K

is for K9 (Canine)

There are over 1,300 military working dog/handler teams worldwide, and all of them have gone through the Air Force military working dogs program. It's there where dogs such as German Shepherds, Dutch Shepherds, and Belgian Malinois are trained to sniff out dangerous materials. These dogs are strong, smart, and most of all, courageous!

L

is for LONGEVITY

Since 1947, the Air Force Longevity Service Award is presented to all service members who complete four years of military service. Bronze and silver oak-leaf clusters are worn on the ribbon to indicate subsequent awards.

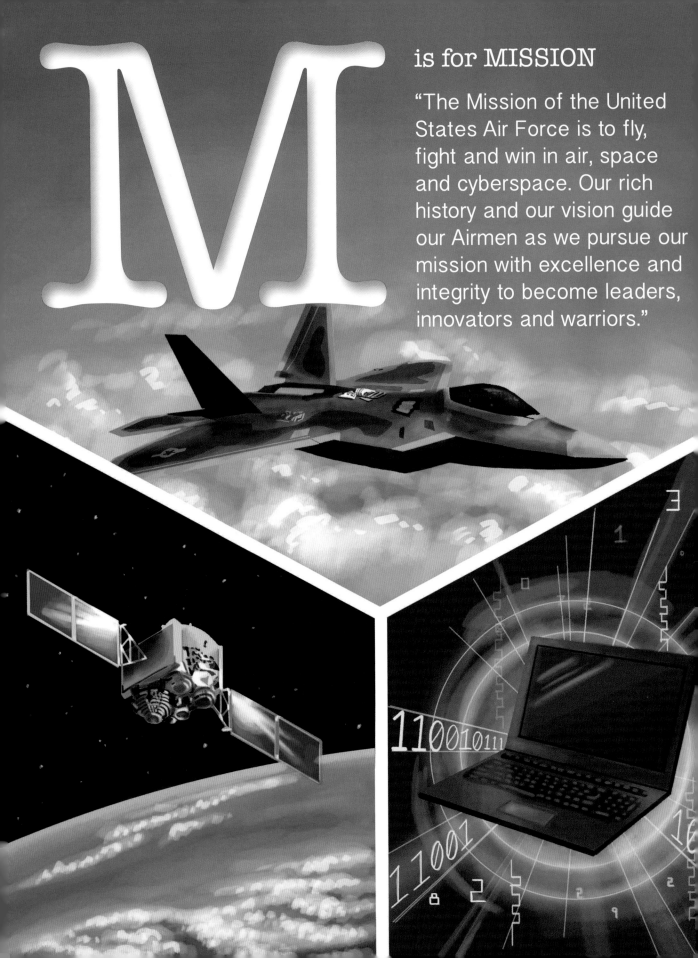

M

is for MISSION

"The Mission of the United States Air Force is to fly, fight and win in air, space and cyberspace. Our rich history and our vision guide our Airmen as we pursue our mission with excellence and integrity to become leaders, innovators and warriors."

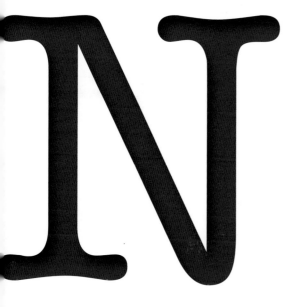

is for NCO
(NON-COMISSIONED
OFFICER)

An Airman who
demonstrates the
leadership and
determination for
promotion becomes an
NCO. That means they
must take care of the
Airmen assigned to them
and lead them well.

is for OFFICER

The officer ranks in the Air Force are:

Second Lieutenant

First Lieutenant

Captain

Major

Lieutenant Colonel

Colonel

Brigadier General

Major General

Lieutenant General

General

P
is for PENTAGON

The Pentagon in Washington, D.C. is where the headquarters of the Air Force is located. It's one of the world's largest office buildings!

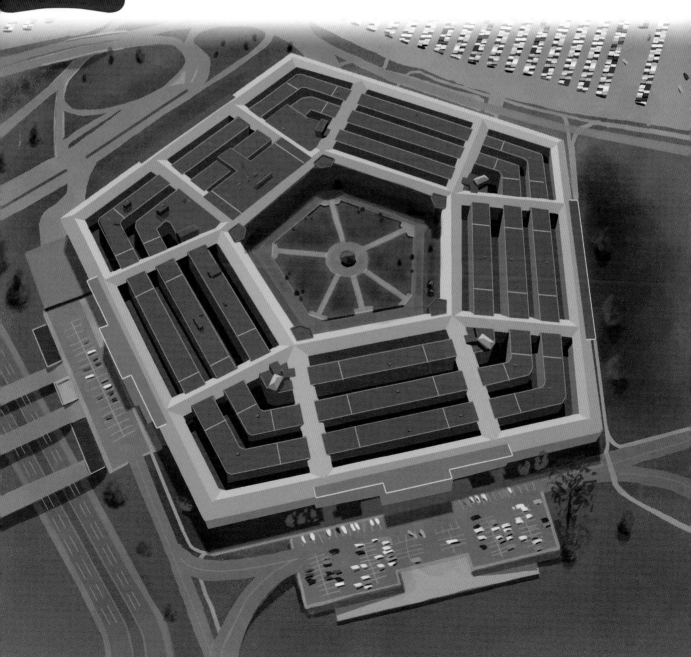

Q is for HAVE QUICK

Have Quick is a system used in Air Force aircraft to protect radio communications. It was designed by electrical engineers to make sure that these communications could not be heard by people who should not be hearing them. Have Quick keeps our airmen safe and secure!

R

is for RESCUE

Pararescuemen, called "PJs" (short for the old term "para-jumpers"), fly to remote locations to rescue Airmen in need. They're highly trained and know just what to do "that others may live!"

S is for SPECIALTY

Each Airman has a special job with a number called an Air Force Specialty Code. These jobs become careers and there are over 200 careers to choose from!

T

is for TRAFFIC

Air traffic controllers provide safe flow of air traffic using their eyes and radar. They can operate on base or in remote places to direct air traffic for special operations.

U

is for UAV (UNMANNED AERIAL VEHICLE)

The UAV helps the Air Force know what is going on from a distance by providing real-time video. These videos are used to help the Air Force's missions succeed.

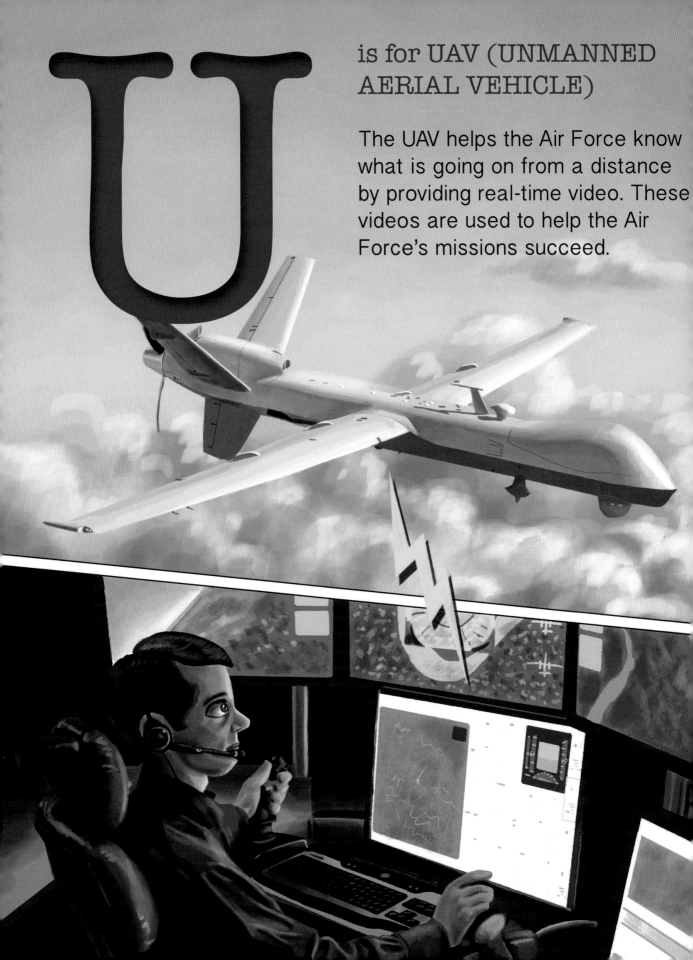

V

is for VISION

The Air Force Vision statement is: "The World's Greatest Air Force—Powered by Airmen, Fueled by Innovation. Through shared values, key capabilities and upholding our Airman's Creed, we continue to achieve our mission and aim high in all we do."

W

is for WINGMAN

In the Air Force, each Airman has a partner, or wingman. Every Airman is taught to always take care of their wingman.

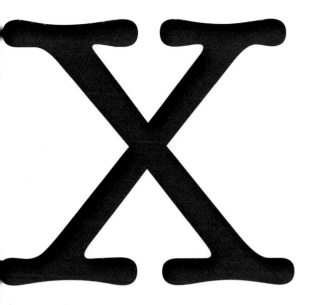

X

is for X-RAY

Airmen use the phonetic alphabet to make sure others know what they are saying. In the phonetic alphabet, each letter is represented by a word. For X, Airmen say "x-ray."

A - Alfa
B - Bravo
C - Charlie
D - Delta
E - Echo
F - Foxtrot
G - Golf
H - Hotel
I - India
J - Juliet
K - Kilo
L - Lima
M - Mike

N - November
O - Oscar
P - Papa
Q - Quebec
R - Romeo
S - Sierra
T - Tango
U - Uniform
V - Victor
W - Whisky
X - X-ray
Y - Yankee
Z - Zulu

Y

is for YONDER

The words to the first verse
of the Air Force song are:
"Off we go into the wild
blue yonder,
Climbing high into the sun...
Hey!
Nothing can stop the U.S.
Air Force!"

Z

is for ZULU

When Air Force members need a way to make sure that events happen at the same time everywhere in the world, they use Zulu time. Sometimes it's called "Greenwich Mean Time" because Zulu time is always the current time in Greenwich, England!

About the Author

Richard Lee Marsh (aka Dick, Norm, or Swamp Thing)
served the USAF for over 34 years as a civilian, a
contractor, a member of the Air National Guard, the
Air Force Reserve, and the Regular Air Force. He
sees those years as his BEST ever and "would love
to do it all over again."

Have a book idea?

Contact us at:

info@mascotbooks.com | www.mascotbooks.com